BARBRA STREISAND

The Voice of a Generation - A Comprehensive Exploration of the Iconic Singer

Stacy B. Brown

TABLE OF CONTENTS

INTRODUCTION

Barbra Streisand is a name that is associated with talent, adaptability, and unrivaled artistic ability. Through her distinguished lifetime crossing north of sixty years, she has made a permanent imprint on the universes of music, film, theater, and activism. With her obvious voice, ordering stage presence, and diverse gifts as a vocalist, entertainer, and chief, Streisand has dazzled crowds all over the planet and solidified her status as a genuine symbol of amusement.

Conceived Barbara Joan Streisand on April 24, 1942, in Brooklyn, New York, she experienced childhood in humble environmental factors with her mom Diana, a teacher, and her stepfather Louis, a secondary school English educator. Since the beginning, Streisand showed a characteristic style for performing, frequently engaging her family with unrehearsed singing and emotional recitations.

Regardless of confronting monetary difficulties and familial difficulties, Streisand's assurance and desire pushed her forward. She sharpened her art in neighborhood ability shows and local area theaters, displaying her crude ability and unquestionable magnetism. It was obvious and still, at the end of the day that she had an uncommon gift — a voice that could easily take off to stunning levels while conveying a profundity of feeling that resounded with crowds on a significant level.

Streisand's advancement came in 1962 when she handled the lead job of Fanny Brice in the Broadway melodic "Amusing Young Lady." Her entrancing exhibition procured her basic praise and sent off her into superstardom for all intents and purposes for the time being. With her dynamic stage presence and stalwart vocals, Streisand spellbound crowds many evenings, procuring a Tony Grant for her depiction of Brice.

Streisand seamlessly made the transition from Broadway to film, where she continued to demonstrate her remarkable talent and versatility. Her film debut in "Entertaining Young Lady" (1968), repeating her job as Fanny Brice, procured her a Foundation Grant for Best Entertainer — an accomplishment essentially unfathomable for a newbie to the cinema. Streisand proceeded to convey a line of notable exhibitions in movies, for example, "Hi, Cart!" (1969), "How We Were" (1973), and "A Star Is Conceived" (1976), cementing her status as perhaps of Hollywood's most venerated driving woman.

Past her achievements as a vocalist and entertainer, Streisand has likewise made critical commitments as a chief, maker, and lobbyist. She broke unattainable ranks in a male-overwhelmed industry, becoming perhaps the earliest lady to compose, direct, produce, and star in her movies. Streisand's obligation to civil rights and moderate causes has been similarly great, utilizing her foundation to advocate for LGBTQ+ privileges, natural protection, and orientation balance.

This comprehensive look at Barbra Streisand's life and work delves deeply into her achievements, setbacks, and lasting legacy. From her unassuming starting points in Brooklyn to her transient ascent to notoriety, and from her earth-shattering accomplishments in amusement to her energetic activism and magnanimity, Streisand's process is exceptional. Go along with us as we praise the life and tradition of an opposed lady show, broken obstructions, and made a permanent imprint on the world stage: Barbra Streisand.

CHAPTER 1: EARLY LIFE AND Adolescence

Barbra Streisand's excursion to fame started in the unassuming environmental factors of Brooklyn, New York, where she was brought into the world on April 24, 1942. As the little girl of Diana and Emanuel Streisand, she encountered a youth set apart by monetary battles and familial difficulties. Diana, her mother, was left to raise her on her own after her father passed away when she was just 15 months old. Diana remarried to Louis Kind, who became a mentor to Barbra and her more established sibling, Sheldon.

Streisand was born with a natural talent for performing and a voracious appetite for knowledge. Regardless of her family's restricted assets, she tracked down comfort and motivation in books, music, and human expression. Streisand's early years were shaped by her mother's support and encouragement, which helped her develop her talent and creativity.

Streisand was exposed to a melting pot of influences as a child in Brooklyn's culturally diverse neighborhoods, which would later influence her eclectic style and artistic sensibilities. She went to Erasmus Lobby Secondary

School, where her unpredictable looks and frank disposition put her aside from her companions. Despite confronting mocking and dismissal for not adjusting to conventional norms of magnificence, Streisand stayed undaunted in her faith in herself and her capacities.

During her young years, Streisand found her energy for performing and started sharpening her specialty in nearby ability shows and local area theaters. Her unmistakable voice and directing stage presence grabbed the eye of crowds and industry insiders the same, laying the foundation for her future achievement.

Streisand faced challenges on her way to stardom despite her growing talent. She battled with sensations of weakness and self-question, wrestling with the tensions of cultural assumptions and the unforgiving real factors of the entertainment biz. However, it was unequivocally these provokes that filled her assurance to succeed and pushed her towards significance.

Streisand's early stages were portrayed by a constant quest for greatness and a refusal to be restricted by the impediments forced by others. She drew motivation from her environmental factors, directing her encounters of affliction and flexibility into her imaginativeness. It was this legitimacy and crude weakness that would eventually separate her as an entertainer and charm her to crowds all over the planet.

As we dig further into Barbra Streisand's initial life and adolescence, we uncover the developmental encounters and impacts that formed the direction of her uncommon excursion. From the roads of Brooklyn to the splendid lights of Broadway, Streisand's resolute assurance and endless ability would impel her towards a predetermination that would everlastingly change the scene of diversion.

1.1 Family History

Barbra Streisand's family history had a significant impact on both her identity and her rise to stardom. Conceived Barbara Joan Streisand on April 24, 1942, in Brooklyn, New York, she was the second offspring of Diana and Emanuel Streisand. Emanuel, a secondary teacher, died from the complexities of an epileptic seizure when Barbra was only 15 months old, passing on Diana to raise her and her more established sibling, Sheldon, as a single parent.

Following Emanuel's passing, Diana remarried to Louis Kind, who turned into an essential figure in Barbra's life. Louis, likewise a secondary teacher, gave security and backing to the family, encouraging a climate where Barbra's imaginative soul could prosper. Regardless of the difficulties of mixing two families and exploring monetary requirements, Diana and Louis made a cherishing and sustaining home for Barbra and her sibling.

Barbra's relationship with her mother, Diana, had a significant impact on her sense of self, strong work ethic, and determination to succeed. Diana, a teacher enthusiastically for writing and human expression, perceived Barbra's extraordinary ability since the beginning and urged her to tirelessly seek after her fantasies.

While Barbra's close family gave a strong groundwork, her more distant family likewise assumed a huge part in molding her personality and perspective. Coming from a Jewish foreign foundation, Streisand was profoundly impacted by her social legacy and childhood. She drew motivation from the rich practices and values that went down through the ages, integrating components of her Jewish character into her imaginativeness and activism.

Streisand has always paid tribute to her roots in her work, incorporating themes of perseverance, resilience, and social justice. Her association with her family and legacy has stayed a steady wellspring of solidarity and motivation, mooring her during the hurricane of distinction and achievement.

As we dig into Barbra Streisand's family foundation, we gain an understanding of the developmental encounters and impacts that formed her into the famous figure she is today. Streisand's upbringing laid the groundwork for a remarkable journey that was marked by creativity, passion, and an unwavering commitment to excellence. This journey laid the foundation for Streisand's remarkable career.

2.2 Youth Battles and Impacts

Barbra Streisand's life as a youngster was set apart by a combination of battles, strength, and powerful encounters that would shape her into the famous figure she is today. Experiencing childhood in Brooklyn, New York, during the 1940s and 1950s, Streisand confronted various difficulties that tried to her purpose and assurance from the beginning.

Quite possibly the main battle Streisand faced during her young life was the deficiency of her dad, Emanuel Streisand, when she was only a little child. Diana Streisand, Streisand's mother, was left to raise Streisand and her older brother, Sheldon, by herself after Emanuel passed away suddenly from complications of an epileptic seizure. This early loss of her dad significantly affected Streisand, molding her point of view and imparting in her a feeling of strength and freedom.

Experiencing childhood in a humble family, Streisand's family confronted monetary difficulties that were frequently gotten by testing to meet. Regardless of these limitations, Streisand's mom, Diana, worked vigorously as a teacher to accommodate her youngsters, imparting in them the worth of difficult work, assurance, and steadiness. Streisand's childhood in this climate of creativity and versatility would later become fundamental to her hard-working attitude and drive for progress.

Streisand's life as a youngster was likewise portrayed by a feeling of otherness and pariah status. With her unusual looks, straightforward disposition, and free thinker mentality, she frequently felt like a nonconformist among her friends. Streisand found solace and escape in the world of books, music, and the arts after she was bullied and ridiculed for not conforming to traditional standards of beauty. She discovered her love of performing and began honing her skills as an actress and singer through these avenues.

Streisand's childhood was also marked by influential experiences that would shape her artistic sensibilities and worldview, despite the difficulties she faced. Experiencing childhood in the socially different neighborhoods of Brooklyn presented her with a blend of impacts, from jazz and blues to Broadway and traditional music. Streisand's varied taste and wide scope of impacts would later become signs of her unmistakable style and creative adaptability.

We learn more about Barbra Streisand's early struggles and influences as we reflect on them. These experiences helped shape her into the iconic figure she is today. From the difficulty she looked to the persuasive encounters that started her energy for execution, Streisand's excursion from humble starting points to worldwide fame is a demonstration of the force of versatility, assurance, and steadfast self-conviction.

CHAPTER 2: ASCEND TO POPULARITY

Barbra Streisand's excursion to popularity is a demonstration of ability, constancy, and an enduring faith in oneself. Streisand's rise to fame is a tale of resilience, determination, and unparalleled artistry, from her humble beginnings in Brooklyn, New York, to her meteoric rise to superstardom on Broadway and beyond.

When Streisand was given the lead role of Fanny Brice in the Broadway musical "Funny Girl" in 1962, it was her big break. At that point, Streisand was a moderately obscure entertainer with restricted proficient experience, however, her tryout had an enduring impact on the show's makers, who were dazzled by her crude ability and attractive stage presence.

"Entertaining Young Lady" was an essential second in Streisand's profession, impelling her into the spotlight and procuring her far and wide praise for her stalwart exhibition. Her version of notable tunes like "Individuals" and "Don't Spoil My Otherwise Good Mood" displayed her unprecedented vocal reach, profound profundity, and unrivaled capacity to order the stage.

Streisand's depiction of Fanny Brice procured her a Tony Grant for Best Entertainer in a Melodic, making her a mind-blowing phenomenon and hardening her status as quite possibly one of Broadway's most splendid stars. Streisand rose to national prominence thanks to the success of her song "Funny Girl," which led to numerous appearances on television and a recording contract with Columbia Records.

With her freshly discovered popularity, Streisand progressed flawlessly into the universe of music, delivering a progression of widely praised collections that exhibited her flexibility as a singer and mediator of melody. Her presentation collection, "The Barbra Streisand Collection" (1963), procured her two Grammy Grants, including Collection of the Year, and laid out her as a considerable power in the music business.

In 1968, Streisand got back to the job of Fanny Brice for the film transformation of "Amusing Young Lady," repeating her Tony Grant-winning execution in the cinema. Her presentation in the film procured her a Foundation Grant for Best Entertainer, making her the solitary entertainer to win both a Tony and an Oscar for a similar job.

Following her outcome in "Entertaining Young Lady," Streisand kept on ruling both the stage and screen, conveying a line of notorious exhibitions in movies, for example, "Hi, Cart!" (A Star Is Born (1976), "The Way We Were" (1973), and With every job, Streisand pushed the limits of her specialty, establishing her status as quite possibly of Hollywood's most respected driving woman.

As we ponder Barbra Streisand's ascent to notoriety, we are helped to remember the groundbreaking force of ability, tirelessness, and the boldness to seek after one's fantasies. From her modest starting points in Brooklyn to her victories on Broadway and then some, Streisand's process is a demonstration of getting through the tradition of a genuine symbol of diversion.

2.1 Starting Points in Amusement

Barbra Streisand's excursion into the universe of diversion started in the energetic neighborhoods of Brooklyn, New York, where her regular ability and attractive mystique put her aside from early on. Despite confronting monetary battles and familial difficulties, Streisand's energy for performing consumed brilliantly, driving her towards a profession that would make a permanent imprint on the universes of music, film, and theater.

From her earliest recollections, Streisand showed an intelligent style for the emotional, frequently engaging her loved ones with off-the-cuff exhibitions and dramatic showcases. Favored with a strong voice and a natural capacity to pass feeling on through tune, Streisand's ability was clear even in her early stages.

Her first experience with the universe of diversion came through nearby ability shows and local area theaters, where she sharpened her art and started to develop her remarkable imaginative voice. Despite her childhood and relative freshness, Streisand's crude ability and unquestionable stage presence grabbed the eye of crowds and industry insiders the same, portending the phenomenal profession that lay ahead.

Diana Streisand, Streisand's mother, recognized her daughter's exceptional talent and constantly encouraged her to pursue her dreams. She was one of Streisand's early influences. Diana, a teacher enthusiastically for writing and human expression, imparted in Streisand an affection for narrating and worship for the groundbreaking force of execution.

As Streisand entered her young years, her energy for performing just extended, and she started to search for open doors to exhibit her ability on a bigger stage. When she won a local YMCA singing contest in 1955, she got her big break by performing at a nightclub in Manhattan's Greenwich Village. The experience was groundbreaking for Streisand, affirming her craving to seek a lifelong diversion and giving her a brief look at the brilliant lights of Broadway.

In the years that followed, Streisand kept on sharpening her specialty, concentrating on acting and singing at the renowned Erasmus Corridor Secondary School and later at New York City's Secondary School of Music and Workmanship. She immersed herself in New York City's vibrant cultural scene, taking in the city's theaters, jazz clubs, and art galleries for inspiration.

Streisand's early experiences in the entertainment industry gave her the skills, self-assurance, and drive to overcome the obstacles of a competitive industry, laying the groundwork for her subsequent success. As she left on her excursion towards fame, Streisand conveyed with her the illustrations gained from her modest starting points in Brooklyn — a savage hard-working attitude, a steady quest for greatness, and a faithful confidence in the extraordinary force of workmanship.

2.2 Broadway Forward leap

Barbra Streisand's Broadway advancement is an essential section in the narrative of her ascent to fame, denoting the second when her uncommon ability and evident charm caught the hearts of crowds and slung her to public unmistakable quality. Streisand's excursion to Broadway started with her tryout for the lead job of Fanny Brice in the melodic "Entertaining Young Lady," a job that wouldn't just exhibit her colossal vocal ability yet in addition cement her status as a genuine star.

In 1962, at 20 years old, Streisand tried out for the job of Fanny Brice in "Entertaining Young Lady" with minimal expert experience yet an abundance of crude ability and irrefutable presence. Despite confronting suspicion from the show's makers because of her flighty looks and absence of Broadway experience, Streisand's tryout had an enduring impression, with her strong voice and attractive stage presence separating her from the opposition.

In "Funny Girl," Streisand's performance as Fanny Brice was nothing short of revelatory. With her unparalleled vocal range, emotional depth, and comedic timing, Streisand gave the character new life. From the second she ventured onto the stage, Streisand told the crowd's consideration, imbuing each line and verse with a substantial feeling of energy and realness.

"Amusing Young Lady" debuted on Broadway at the Colder Time of Year Nursery Theater on Walk 26, 1964, to rave surveys and heartfelt applauses. Critics and viewers alike gave Streisand's performance high marks, hailing her as a once-in-a-generation talent. Her version of famous tunes like "Individuals" and "Don't Spoil My Otherwise Good Mood" became moment works of art, procuring her a Tony Grant for Best Entertainer in a Melodic and hardening her status as perhaps of Broadway's most splendid star.

Streisand's outcome in "Entertaining Young Lady" denoted a defining moment in her profession, making the way for a universe of chances in film, music, and then some. Her attractive presentation shot her to public conspicuousness, prompting various TV appearances, recording agreements, and film offers.

In addition to achieving commercial success, Streisand's performance in "Funny Girl" established new ground for women working in the entertainment industry by challenging conventional gender roles and laying the groundwork for future generations of female performers. Streisand's depiction of Fanny Brice as a solid, free lady with organization and desire reverberated with crowds, making her a pioneer by her own doing.

We are reminded of the transformative power of talent, perseverance, and the courage to pursue one's dreams as we reflect on Barbra Streisand's Broadway breakthrough. Streisand's journey is a testament to the lasting legacy of a true entertainment icon, from her humble beginnings in Brooklyn to her triumphs on Broadway.

CHAPTER 3: ENTERTAINING YOUNG LADY" AND FAME

Barbra Streisand's depiction of Fanny Brice in the melodic "Amusing Young Lady" denoted the start of her climb to superstardom and hardened her status as perhaps one of the most famous figures in amusement history. The outcome of "Amusing Young Lady" on Broadway and its ensuing transformation to the cinema impelled Streisand into the spotlight, acquiring her far and wide approval and reverence from crowds all over the planet.

"Amusing Young Lady" appeared on Broadway at the Colder time of year Nursery Theater on Walk 26, 1964, with Streisand in the number one spot job of Fanny Brice. The melodic, with music by Jule Styne, verses by Bounce Merrill, and a book by Isobel Lennart, recounts the tale of Fanny Brice, a Jewish young lady from the Lower East Side of New York who ascends to distinction as a vaudeville star regardless of confronting various individual and expert difficulties.

Streisand's presentation as Fanny Brice was completely dramatic, procuring her rave surveys and a Tony Grant for Best Entertainer in a Melodic. Her dynamic stage presence, stalwart vocals, and faultless comedic timing rejuvenated the personality of Fanny Brice such that enraptured crowds for a large number of evenings.

The progress of "Entertaining Young Lady" on Broadway prepared for its variation to the cinema, with Streisand repeating her job as Fanny Brice in the 1968 film transformation. Coordinated by William Wyler, the film was a basic and business achievement, procuring Streisand a Foundation Grant for Best Entertainer — an uncommon accomplishment for a novice to the universe of film.

Streisand's presentation in "Entertaining Young Lady" launched her to superstardom, making her an easily recognized name and hardening her status as quite possibly one of Hollywood's most pursued driving women. With her particular voice, striking magnificence, and attractive stage presence, Streisand enthralled crowds all over the planet, turning into a social symbol and an image of female strengthening.

"Funny Girl," in addition to having an impact on Streisand's career, challenged conventional gender roles and celebrated female ambition and independence. It also set new standards for women in the entertainment industry. With audiences of all ages and backgrounds, Streisand's portrayal of Fanny Brice as a strong, tenacious woman who defied expectations and pursued her dreams on her terms cemented her legacy as a trailblazer and an inspiration to generations of performers.

We are reminded of the transformative power of talent, perseverance, and the courage to defy convention as we reflect on Barbra Streisand's rise to fame with "Funny Girl." Streisand's journey is a testament to the lasting legacy of a true entertainment icon, from her Broadway debut to her triumphs on the big screen.

3.1 Job of Fanny Brice

Fanny Brice, deified by Barbra Streisand's notorious depiction, is a person whose intricacy, flexibility, and enthusiastic soul have enthralled crowds for ages. In both the Broadway melodic "Entertaining Young Lady" and its film transformation, Fanny Brice fills in as the substance of the story, an amazing figure whose excursion from humble starting points to fame is both motivating and profoundly human.

At its center, Fanny Brice's personality epitomizes the quintessential American dream — an untouchable with huge dreams and a much greater character who opposes the chance to make progress in her specific manner. Naturally introduced to destitution in New York City's Lower East Side, Fanny Brice transcends her conditions through sheer ability, assurance, and a steady confidence in herself.

Fanny Brice is best known for her unstoppable spirit and infectious sense of humor. Regardless of confronting various difficulties and difficulties all through her profession, Fanny's fast mind, harsh tone, and disrespectful comical inclination act as both a guard system and a wellspring of solidarity. Her capacity to giggle even with misfortune charms her to crowds and assists her with exploring the promising and less promising times of life on the stage.

Integral to Fanny Brice's personality is her relationship with Scratch Arnstein, an enchanting player and running woman's man who becomes both her darling and her most noteworthy cause of despair. Their turbulent sentiment frames the close-to-home center of "Entertaining Young Lady," as Fanny wrestles with the intricacies of affection, desire, and self-esteem. Regardless of the obstructions they face, Fanny's affection for Scratch stays unflinching, even as she figures out how to take care of herself and seek after her fantasies autonomous of him.

At its heart, Fanny Brice's process is one of self-disclosure and strengthening. All through "Entertaining Young Lady," she wrestles with issues of personality, self-esteem, and the quest for satisfaction, at last tracking down satisfaction not in that frame of mind of a man, but rather in the acknowledgment of her true capacity as an entertainer and as a lady. Fanny's victories and hardships reflect those of endless ladies who have considered challenging shows and outlined their course in a world that frequently tries to restrict their desires. Fanny Brice is beautifully portrayed by Barbra Streisand, who brings the character's larger-than-life personality, vulnerability, and unwavering spirit to life with unrivaled depth and authenticity. Through her nuanced execution, Streisand rejuvenates Fanny Brice in the entirety of her intricacy, making her an engaging and persevering figure whose excursion keeps on reverberating with crowds of any age and foundation.

Fanny Brice is, in the end, more than just a character; she is also a representation of perseverance, strength, and the strength of self-belief. Her inheritance lives on in the hearts and brains of all who have been enlivened by her excursion, advising us that sincerely, boldness, and a tad of humor, the sky is the limit.

3.2 Basic Praise and Grants

Barbra Streisand's unrivaled ability and weighty exhibitions have procured her far and wide basic praise and various honors all through her famous lifetime. From her initial victories on Broadway to her notorious jobs in the cinema, Streisand's commitments to the universe of diversion have been perceived and celebrated by pundits, friends, and crowds the same.

Streisand's most memorable significant acknowledgment accompanied her Tony Grant win for Best Entertainer in a Melodic for her depiction of Fanny Brice in the Broadway creation of "Interesting Young Lady" in 1964. Her dynamic exhibition, stalwart vocals, and attractive stage presence spellbound crowds and pundits the same, acquiring her rave audits and setting her status as quite possibly one of Broadway's most brilliant stars.

Following her victory on Broadway, Streisand progressed consistently into the universe of the film, where she kept on collecting basic praise for her groundbreaking exhibitions. She won an Academy Award for Best Actress in 1968 for her role as Fanny Brice in the movie version of "Funny Girl," a first for a newcomer to the film industry.

Streisand's progress in "Entertaining Young Lady" made ready for a line of notable exhibitions in movies, for example, "Hi, Cart!" (1969), "How We Were" (1973), and "A Star Is Conceived" (1976), among others. Her capacity to possess a great many characters with profundity, subtlety, and validness procured her far-reaching acclaim from pundits and crowds the same, solidifying her status as perhaps one of Hollywood's most worshipped driving women.

Notwithstanding her prosperity in front of an audience and screen, Streisand has likewise delighted in enormous accomplishment as a recording craftsman, procuring various Grammy Grants for her commitments to the universe of music. Her presentation collection, "The Barbra Streisand Collection" (1963), procured her two Grammy Grants, including Collection of the Year, denoting the start of a celebrated vocation that has traversed north of sixty years.

All through her profession, Streisand has been perceived with incalculable honors and respects, including different Emmy Grants, Brilliant Globe Grants, and an Official Decoration of Opportunity. Her effect on the universes of music, film, and activism has been tremendous, procuring her an extremely durable spot in the pantheon of diversion legends.

As we consider Barbra Streisand's basic praise and grants, we are helped to remember the extraordinary force of ability, steadiness, and the mental fortitude to seek after one's fantasies. From her momentous exhibitions on Broadway to her notable jobs in the cinema, Streisand's inheritance is a demonstration of the force of masterfulness and the unstoppable soul of a genuine symbol.

CHAPTER 4: CAREER IN FILM

Barbra Streisand's film career demonstrates her versatility, talent, and lasting influence on the film industry. From her initial triumphs in melodic comedies to her historic work as a chief, Streisand's commitments to the cinema have procured her boundless recognition and set her status as quite possibly of Hollywood's most venerated driving woman.

Streisand's movie profession started decisively with her job as Fanny Brice in the 1968 film variation of "Amusing Young Lady." Coordinated by William Wyler, the film procured Streisand an Institute Grant for Best Entertainer, making her the sole entertainer to win both a Tony and an Oscar for a similar job. Streisand's dynamic presentation and stalwart vocals enthralled crowds and pundits the same, laying out her as an awe-inspiring phenomenon in the realm of film.

Following the outcome of "Entertaining Young Lady," Streisand proceeded to exhibit her gifts in different jobs, procuring basic praise for her exhibitions in movies, for example, "Hi, Cart!" (A Star Is Born (1976), "The Way We Were" (1973), and Streisand displayed her remarkable versatility as an actress in each of these films by effortlessly and precisely transitioning between musical theater, comedy, and drama.

Streisand made significant contributions behind the scenes as a director, producer, and writer in addition to her work as an actress. In 1983, she made her first time at the helm with the film "Yentl," an earth-shattering melodic show about a youthful Jewish lady who camouflages herself as a man to seek after her fantasies about concentrating on Writing. " Yentl" procured Streisand basic recognition and various honors, including a Brilliant Globe for Best Chief — a noteworthy accomplishment for a female movie producer at that point.

All through her vocation, Streisand has kept on pushing the limits of her creativity, handling testing and provocative jobs that challenge cultural standards, and praipraising force of flexibility and self-revelation. Whether on screen or behind the camera, Streisand's obligation to greatness and her resolute commitment to her specialty has made her a genuine pioneer and a motivation to ages of entertainers.

As we consider Barbra Streisand's movie profession, we are helped to remember the extraordinary force of narrating and the persevering effect of a genuine craftsman. From her leading-edge job in "Amusing

Young Lady" to her noteworthy work as a chief, Streisand's inheritance in the realm of film is a demonstration of the perseverance force of film to engage, move, and incite thought.

4.1 Acting Features

Barbra Streisand's acting vocation is a demonstration of her flexibility, ability, and capacity to possess a large number of characters with profundity, subtlety, and legitimacy. From her initial accomplishments in melodic comedies to her later emotional jobs, Streisand's exhibitions on screen have acquired her far and wide praise and set her status as quite possibly one of Hollywood's most venerated driving women.

One of Streisand's most notable jobs came right off the bat in her vocation with her depiction of Fanny Brice in the 1968 film transformation of "Entertaining Young Lady." Coordinated by William Wyler, the film procured Streisand a Foundation Grant for Best Entertainer, making her the sole entertainer to win both a Tony and an Oscar for a similar job. Streisand's dynamic presentation and stalwart vocals dazzled crowds and pundits the same, laying out her as an amazing powerhouse in the realm of film.

Following her outcome in "Entertaining Young Lady," Streisand proceeded to grandstand her gifts in different jobs, acquiring basic recognition for her exhibitions in movies, for example, "Hi, Cart!" (A Star Is Conceived

(1976), "How We Were" (1973), and In all of these films, Streisand showed her earth-shattering reach as a performer, perfectly changing between parody, show, and melodic venue with beauty and accuracy.

In "Hi, Cart!" Streisand displayed her comedic gifts as the enthusiastic relational arranger Cart Levi, acquiring acclaim for her immaculate timing and irresistible enthusiasm. In "How We Were," Streisand conveyed a powerful and grievous execution as Katie Morosky, a wildly free lady whose adoration for a politically aggressive man (played by Robert Redford) is tried by the turbulent occasions of the twentieth hundred years. What's more, in "A Star Is Conceived," Streisand stunned crowds with her depiction of Esther Hoffman, a capable vocalist whose ascent to popularity is eclipsed by the reckless way of behaving of her significant other (played by Kris Kristofferson).

Notwithstanding her work in highlight films, Streisand has additionally made huge commitments to the universe of TV, acquiring basic praise for her exhibitions in undertakings, for example, "The Barbra Streisand Extraordinary" (1965), "Barbra Streisand: Ageless" (2001), and "Barbra Streisand... Furthermore, Other Instruments" (1973). Her capacity to spellbind crowds on both the huge what's more, little screens has made her a genuine symbol of diversion and a pioneer for ladies in the business.

We are reminded of the transformative power of storytelling and the lasting impact of a true artist as we reflect on Barbra Streisand's best roles. Streisand's legacy as an actress is a testament to the enduring power of cinema to entertain, inspire, and provoke thought. From her breakthrough role in "Funny Girl" to her diverse body of work that spans decades, Streisand's career is a testament to this power.

4.2 Progress to Coordinating

Barbra Streisand's progress from acting to coordinating denoted an urgent second in her profession, exhibiting her gifts behind the camera and cementing her status as a diverse craftsman. Streisand's introduction to coordinating was described by a strength of vision, a promise to greatness, and an eagerness to challenge shows, bringing about a progression of noteworthy movies that procured her broad praise and acknowledgment as a pioneer in the realm of film.

Streisand's first time at the helm came in 1983 with the film "Yentl," a melodic show in light of the brief tale "Yentl the Yeshiva Kid" by Isaac Bashevis Vocalist. As well as coordinating the film, Streisand likewise featured leading the pack job as Yentl, a youthful Jewish lady who masks herself as a man to seek after her fantasies about concentrating on the Commentary — a considering starting that tested cultural standards and investigated subjects of orientation personality, custom, and self-disclosure.

"Yentl" was a meaningful venture for Streisand, who had been attracted to the story's subjects of female strengthening and the quest for information since she originally found Vocalist's work during the 1960s. Not set in stone to carry the story to the screen with genuineness and trustworthiness, Streisand battled eagerly to get subsidizing for the movie and imaginative command over its creation — an accomplishment that was unbelievable for a female chief at that point.

"Yentl" received widespread critical acclaim upon its release, which led to Streisand receiving numerous awards and nominations, including a Golden Globe for Best Director, a first for a female filmmaker at the time. Pundits adulated Streisand's heading, her nuanced execution as Yentl, and the film's rich cinematography, blending melodic score, and interesting investigation of orientation and personality.

Following the outcome of "Yentl," Streisand kept on pushing the limits of her masterfulness as a chief, helming a different scope of undertakings that displayed her flexibility and inventive vision. Streisand created emotionally resonant stories that resonated with audiences worldwide in films like "The Prince of Tides" (1991), "The Mirror Has Two Faces" (1996), and "Yentl." In each of these films, she dealt with complex themes with sensitivity and depth.

Streisand's move to directing marked a turning point in her career. She was able to explore new ways to tell stories and express herself while continuing to challenge preconceived notions about women working in the film industry and break down barriers. Her prosperity as a chief prepared for people in the future of female movie producers, motivating endless ladies to seek after their fantasies behind the camera.

As we ponder Barbra Streisand's change to coordinating, we are helped to remember the extraordinary force of masterfulness and the getting-through effect of a genuine visionary. From her pivotal presentation with "Yentl" to her different groups of work as a chief, Streisand's heritage in the realm of film is a demonstration of the force of narrating to move, incite thought, and change hearts and brains.

CHAPTER 5: MELODIC ACCOMPLISHMENTS

Barbra Streisand's melodic accomplishments are a demonstration of her unmatched ability, flexibility, and getting through influence on the universe of music. From her initial victories as a Broadway sensation to her weighty work as a recording craftsman, Streisand's commitments to the melodic scene have procured her far-reaching praise and hardened her status as one of the best voices ever.

Streisand's melodic excursion started on the Broadway stage, where she made her leading-edge execution as Fanny Brice in the 1964 melodic "Entertaining Young Lady." Her dynamic vocals, close-to-home profundity, and telling stage presence spellbound crowds and pundits the same, procuring her a Tony Grant for Best Entertainer in a Melodic and sending off her vocation as a real star.

Streisand seamlessly entered the music industry following her Broadway success, releasing a string of critically acclaimed albums that demonstrated her versatility as a singer and song interpreter. "The Barbra Streisand Album," her first album, came out in 1963. It won her two Grammy Awards, including Album of the Year, and made her a powerful force in the music business.

All through her profession, Streisand has kept on pushing the limits of her creativity, investigating a large number of melodic kinds and working together with probably the most praised lyricists, writers, and performers of her age. From Broadway principles and pop ditties to jazz guidelines and contemporary hits, Streisand's collection is however various as it very well might be immortal, interesting to crowds of any age and foundation.

One of Streisand's most prominent accomplishments as a recording craftsman is her unmatched accomplishment on the Board graphs. With over 68.5 million confirmed collections sold in the US alone, Streisand is one of the most mind-blowing selling recording craftsmen ever — a demonstration of the perseverance prevalenthe ce of her music and the unflinching unwaveringness of her fans.

Streisand's effect on the universe of music reaches a long way past her record-breaking deals and graph-besting hits. She has used her music to advocate for social causes, encourage cultural diversity, and inspire positive change throughout her career. From her notable presentation of "How We Were" at the 1974 Foundation Grants to her strong interpretation of "Envision" at the 2001 Emmy Grants, Streisand's music has filled in as an energizing sob for harmony, equity, and balance.

As we ponder Barbra Streisand's melodic accomplishments, we are helped to remember the extraordinary force of imaginativeness and the perseverance effect of a genuine symbol. From her extraordinary exhibitions on Broadway to her immortal accounts and humanitarian undertakings, Streisand's inheritance in the realm of music is a demonstration of the force of ability, tirelessness, and mental fortitude to seek after one's fantasies.

5.1 Collections and Graph Besting Hits

Barbra Streisand's discography is a demonstration of her unrivaled ability, flexibility, and perseverance through her influence on the universe of music. With more than 35 studio collections, 9 live collections, and various accumulation collections to her name, Streisand's commitments to the melodic scene have acquired her far-reaching approval and hardened her status as one of the best voices ever.

"The Barbra Streisand Album," Streisand's first album, came out in 1963. It propelled her to fame and won her two Grammy Awards, including Album of the Year. Including a blend of Broadway guidelines, pop numbers, and jazz works of art, the collection exhibited Streisand's wonderful vocal reach, profound profundity, and interpretive expertise, making way for an unbelievable profession.

All through the 1960s and 1970s, Streisand delivered a line of widely praised collections that cemented her standing as one of the most flexible and persuasive specialists of her age. Collections like "Individuals" (1964), "Interesting Young Lady: Unique Soundtrack Recording" (1968), and "Stoney End" (1971) displayed

Streisand's capacity to flawlessly change among classes and styles, from Broadway show tunes to pop hits to contemporary ditties.

One of Streisand's most famous collections is "Liable" (1980), a joint effort with incredible lyricist Barry Gibb of the Honey Bee Gees. The collection created a few graph-beating hits, including "Lady in Affection" and "Liable," and procured Streisand a Grammy Grant for Best Pop Vocal Execution, Female. " Guilty" has been and continues to be one of Streisand's best-selling albums, establishing her status as a pop music icon. Notwithstanding her prosperity as an independent craftsman, Streisand has likewise made outline finishing off progress with her two-part harmonies and coordinated efforts. Her two-part harmony with Neil Jewel, "You Don't Bring Me Blossoms" (1978), arrived at number one on the Board Hot 100 outline and became one of the most incredible selling singles of the 10 years. Streisand's joint efforts with craftsmen like Celine Dion, Bryan Adams, and Donna Summer have additionally beaten out everyone else and procured her basic recognition for her flexibility and versatility as an entertainer.

Streisand's effect on the music business stretches out a long way past her diagram beating hits and record-breaking deals. All through her vocation, she has utilized her foundation to support social causes, advance social variety, and motivate positive change through her music. From her notorious exhibitions at benefit shows to her charitable undertakings, Streisand's music keeps on filling in as a wellspring of motivation and strengthening for a huge number of fans all over the planet.

As we ponder Barbra Streisand's collections and diagram besting hits, we are helped to remember the extraordinary force of music and the getting-through tradition of a genuine symbol. From her initial triumphs on Broadway to her noteworthy joint efforts and magnanimous endeavors, Streisand's effect on the universe of music is a demonstration of the force of ability, diligence, and the mental fortitude to seek after one's fantasies.

5.3 Impact on Music Industry

Barbra Streisand's impact on the music business is significant and extensive, traversing several decades and types. As one of the most notable and adaptable specialists ever, Streisand's effect can be felt on each side of the music world, from Broadway stages to show lobbies to recording studios. Here are a few vital manners by which Streisand has influenced the music business:

1. Vocal Ability and Creative Uprightness: Streisand's exceptional vocal reach, emotive conveyance, and faultless skill have set the highest quality level for artists across ages. Her capacity to pass feeling on through melody, decipher verses with profundity and subtlety, and order the stage with power has procured her broad approval and profound respect from companions and fans the same.

2. Flexibility and Versatility: All through her vocation, Streisand has shown exceptional flexibility as a craftsman, easily progressing among types and styles effortlessly. From Broadway principles to pop melodies to jazz works of art, Streisand's different collections request to crowds of any age and foundation, exhibiting

her flexibility and resilience in an always evolving industry.

3. Limit Breaking Joint efforts: Some of Streisand's collaborations with other artists have resulted in some of music history's most enduring and iconic songs. Streisand's ability to connect with her musical partners and elevate their performances has established her status as a true collaborator and innovator, whether she collaborates with Barry Gibb on the chart-topping album "Guilty" or performs as a duet with Neil Diamond on the song "You Don't Bring Me Flowers."

4. Effect on Female Strengthening: Streisand's exploring vocation has propelled endless ladies to seek after their fantasies and separate obstructions in the music business. Streisand's accomplishments, which range from her breakthrough role as Fanny Brice in "Funny Girl" to her historic victory as the first female director to win a Golden Globe Award, have paved the way for subsequent generations of female artists, directors, and executives in the entertainment industry.

5. Altruism and Social Activism: Streisand has involved her foundation as a performer and well-known person to advocate for social causes and advance positive change on the planet. Through her beneficent establishment, The Streisand Establishment, she has upheld a large number

of causes, including schooling, ladies' privileges, medical care, and the climate, leaving an enduring tradition of empathy and liberality.

Generally speaking, Barbra Streisand's impact on the music business is inconceivable, contacting the existences of millions of fans and rousing incalculable craftsmen to take a stab at greatness, realness, and social obligation. As an entertainer, partner, and donor, Streisand's effect will keep on reverberating for a long time into the future, guaranteeing her inheritance as one of the best voices ever.

CHAPTER 6: PERSONAL LIFE

Barbra Streisand has a personal life that is just as rich and diverse as her long and illustrious career. From her unassuming starting points in Brooklyn to her status as a social symbol, Streisand's process has been formed by adoration, misfortune, win, and versatility. Here are a few critical parts of Streisand's own life:

1. Early Years and Family: Diana and Emanuel Streisand gave birth to Streisand on April 24, 1942, in Brooklyn, New York. She experienced childhood in an affectionate Jewish family, encompassed by music, writing, and a solid feeling of social character. Regardless of confronting monetary battles and familial difficulties, Streisand's folks imparted in her an adoration for learning and a confidence in the force of dreams.

2. Connections and Marriage: Streisand's heartfelt life has been the subject of many hypotheses and media consideration throughout the long term. She has been hitched two times: She got married twice, first in 1963 to actor Elliott Gould, with whom she had a son named Jason Gould, and then in 1998 to actor James Brolin. Streisand's relationships have been described by adoration, common regard, and a common obligation to

family, notwithstanding the difficulties of life at the center of attention.

3. Parenthood and Family: The role that Streisand has played as a mother has been a major focus of her life, influencing her priorities and career choices. Her child, Jason Gould, has emulated her example as an entertainer and performer, manufacturing his way into media outlets while keeping a nearby bond with his mom. Streisand has been a source of strength and inspiration throughout her life for her dedication to her family and to providing them with a secure and nurturing environment.

4. Activism and Generosity: Streisand's own life is additionally set apart by her energetic obligation to social causes and magnanimity. Through her magnanimous establishment, The Streisand Establishment, she has upheld many causes, including training, ladies' freedoms, medical care, and the climate, leaving an enduring tradition of sympathy and liberality. Streisand's activism mirrors her profoundly held convictions in equity, balance, and the force of individual activity to make positive change on the planet.

5. Heritage and Reflection: As Streisand ponders her own life and vocation, she stays thankful for the potential open doors and encounters that have molded her excursion. From her initial battles in Brooklyn to her

victories on the world stage, Streisand's life is a demonstration of perseverance through the force of versatility, assurance, and the boldness to seek after one's fantasies. As she keeps on motivating crowds all over the planet with her music, movies, and activism, Streisand's inheritance will persevere as an encouraging sign and motivation for a long time into the future.

6.1 Relationships and Connections

Barbra Streisand's heartfelt life has been the subject of much interest and hypothesis throughout the long term, as she explored the ups and downs of affection, marriage, and connections in the public eye. A comprehensive look at Streisand's significant relationships and marriages can be found here:

1. Elliott Gould, born 1963–1971, was: Streisand married actor Elliott Gould, whom she first met in 1962, in her first marriage. The couple secured the bunch on September 14, 1963, and invited their child, Jason Gould, in 1966. Due to their shared passion for acting and the arts, Streisand and Gould were regarded as one of Hollywood's golden couples. Notwithstanding, their marriage confronted difficulties because of their requesting professions and the tensions of acclaim. They separated in 1971 yet stayed in friendly conditions, co-nurturing their child together.

2. Jon Peters (took part in the 1970s): Streisand was momentarily connected with to maker Jon Peters during the 1970s. Their relationship was portrayed by enthusiasm and force, and at the end of the day finished before they could stroll down the path.

3. James Brolin (m. 1998-present): Streisand wed actor James Brolin on July 1, 1998, her second and current marriage. They got together in the middle of the 1990s and quickly became inseparable. Brolin, known for his jobs in movies and TV, carried steadiness and friendship to Streisand's life. Together, they have endured the promising and less promising times of marriage in the public eye, supporting each other through wins and difficulties. Their perseverance through affection and shared regard have made them perhaps one of Hollywood's most dearest couples.

Notwithstanding her relationships, Streisand has been connected to a few high-profile connections throughout the long term, incorporating kinships with performers, entertainers, and political figures. Her own life has been portrayed as a guarantee of family, love, and realness, despite the tensions of popularity and public examination.

As Streisand considers her relationships and connections, she stays appreciative of the love and friendship she has tracked down all through her life. While her heartfelt excursion has been set apart by its portion of difficulties and heartbreaks, Streisand's perseverance through good faith and confidence in the force of affection keep on rousing fans all over the planet.

6.2 Relational intricacies

Barbra Streisand's relational intricacies play a critical impact in shaping her life, vocation, and individual connections. Streisand's family has been there for her every step of the way, from when she was growing up in Brooklyn to when she became a wife and a mother. Here is a definite gander at Streisand's relational intricacies:

1. Adolescence and Childhood: Diana and Emanuel Streisand gave birth to Streisand in Brooklyn, New York, to a close-knit Jewish family. Streisand's parents instilled in her a love of music, literature, and culture, nurtured her creative talents, and encouraged her to pursue her dreams despite their family's difficulties and financial difficulties. Streisand's childhood in a common area gave her a solid feeling of flexibility, genius, and assurance that would work well for her in her future undertakings.

2. Parental Impact: Streisand's relationship with her folks significantly affected her life and profession. Diana, Streisand's mother, was a schoolteacher and an amateur singer. She fostered her daughter's interest in music and encouraged her to pursue her passion for performing. Streisand's dad, Emanuel, functioned as a teacher and passed on when she was only 15 months old, leaving her

with a deep-rooted feeling of yearning and misfortune. Streisand has frequently spoken affectionately of her folks' effect on her creative sensibilities and values, acknowledging them for imparting in her a solid hard-working attitude, a feeling of sympathy, and a promise to civil rights.

3. Kin Connections: Streisand had two half-kin from her dad's past marriage, Roslyn Kind and Sheldon Streisand, who assumed a critical part in her life and profession. Roslyn Streisand, Streisand's sister, is also a talented singer and performer. Throughout their lives, the two siblings have supported one another through the highs and lows of their respective careers. Streisand's sibling, Sheldon, died unfortunately in 1972, abandoning a tradition of affection and affectionate recollections.

4. Conjugal and Parental Elements: Streisand's relationships and connections have likewise impacted her relational intricacies throughout the long term. Her most memorable union with entertainer Elliott Gould brought about the introduction of their child, Jason Gould, in 1966. Streisand's job as a mother has been a focal point of her life, forming her needs and impacting her professional decisions. Regardless of the difficulties of offsetting parenthood with her requesting vocation, Streisand has stayed given to her child, Jason, supporting

him in his imaginative interests and sustaining their cozy relationship.

In general, Streisand's identity, values, and outlook on the world have all been heavily influenced by the dynamics in her family. From her childhood in Brooklyn to her encounters as a spouse, mother, and sister, Streisand's family has furnished her with a solid groundwork of adoration, backing, and motivation that keeps on impacting her life and profession right up to the present day.

CHAPTER 7: ACTIVISM AND GENEROSITY

Barbra Streisand's activism and generosity have been fundamental to her personality and heritage, exhibiting her obligation to civil rights, philanthropic causes, and the force of individual activity to make positive change on the planet. All through her profession, Streisand has involved her foundation as a performer, entertainer, and person of note to advocate for many issues, from ladies' privileges to medical care to natural preservation. An in-depth look at Streisand's activism and charitable work can be found here:

1. Rights of Women: Streisand has been a vocal backer for ladies' freedoms all through her vocation, utilizing her foundation to advance orientation fairness and enable ladies to seek after their fantasies. As well as standing up on issues, for example, equivalent compensation and regenerative privileges, Streisand has upheld associations like Arranged Being a Parent and the Public Association for Ladies (Presently), which work to propel ladies' freedoms and potentially open doors.

2. Healthcare: Streisand has been a lifelong fan of medical services change and admittance to reasonable medical care for all Americans. She has given

generously to healthcare and medical research institutions, including the Cedars-Sinai Women's Heart Center in Los Angeles, which is named after her. Streisand's magnanimity in the medical care area has assisted with working on clinical considerations and saving lives all over the planet.

3. LGBTQ+ Privileges: Streisand has for some time been a partner and backer for the LGBTQ+ people group, utilizing her foundation to bring issues to light about issues like marriage correspondence, hostility to segregation regulations, and HIV/Helps counteraction and treatment. She has upheld associations like the Common Freedoms Mission and the Elton John Helps Establishment, which works to progress LGBTQ+ privileges and offer help to people and families impacted by HIV/Helps.

4. Education: Streisand is a major area of strength for instruction and proficiency drives, accepting that admittance to quality schooling is fundamental for enabling people and building more grounded networks. She has given to schools, libraries, and instructive projects all over the planet, assisting with giving assets and amazing open doors to kids and grown-ups the same.

5. Conservation of Nature: Streisand has been a vocal promoter of ecological protection and manageability,

utilizing her foundation to bring issues to light about environmental change, contamination, and natural surroundings obliteration. She has upheld associations like the Normal Assets Guard Chamber (NRDC) and the Ecological Safeguard Asset (EDF), which work to safeguard the planet and protect regular assets for people in the future.

In general, Streisand's activism and altruism mirror her profoundly held upsides of sympathy, equity, and social obligation. Through her liberal gifts, backing endeavors, and public activism, Streisand lastingly affects the world, rousing others to join her in the battle for an all the more, evenhanded, and practical future.

7.1 Causes Upheld

Barbra Streisand's magnanimous endeavors have contacted a great many causes and associations, mirroring her obligation to civil rights, philanthropy, and the improvement of society. All through her vocation, Streisand has utilized her foundation and monetary assets to help causes that line up with her qualities and convictions. Here is a definite gander at a portion of the causes Streisand has upheld:

1. Ladies' Freedoms: Streisand has been an energetic backer of ladies' privileges, supporting associations that work to propel orientation uniformity, conceptive freedoms, and financial strengthening for ladies. She has given to organizations that work to protect and promote women's rights and opportunities, such as Planned Parenthood, the National Organization for Women (NOW), and the Women's Media Center.

2. Healthcare: Streisand has been a liberal ally of medical services drives and clinical exploration, especially in the space of ladies' wellbeing and coronary illness. She has given to clinical examination foundations, clinics, and medical care associations, including the Cedars-Sinai Ladies' Heart Community in

Los Angeles, which is named in her honor. Streisand's magnanimity in the medical services area has assisted with working on clinical considerations and saving lives all over the planet.

3. Rights of the LGBTQ+ community: Streisand has for some time been a partner and backer for the LGBTQ+ people group, supporting associations that work to progress LGBTQ+ freedoms, offer help to people and families impacted by HIV/Helps, and advance acknowledgment and incorporation. She has given money to GLAAD, the Elton John AIDS Foundation, and the Human Rights Campaign, all of which work to make the world a better place for LGBTQ+ people.

4. Education: Streisand is an area of strength for training and proficiency drives, accepting that admittance to quality schooling is fundamental for enabling people and building more grounded networks. She has given to schools, libraries, and instructive projects all over the planet, giving assets and open doors to kids and grown-ups the same. Streisand's help for instruction has assisted with further developing proficiency rates, growing admittance to instructive open doors, and advancing deep-rooted learning.

5. Ecological Preservation: Streisand is a vocal supporter of ecological preservation and manageability, supporting

associations that work to safeguard the planet and protect regular assets for people in the future. She has given to associations like the Regular Assets Guard Board (NRDC), the Natural Safeguard Asset (EDF), and the Sierra Club, which work to address environmental change, safeguard jeopardized species, and advance ecological stewardship.

In general, Barbra Streisand's magnanimous endeavors mirror her profoundly held upsides of empathy, equity, and social obligation. Through her liberal gifts, promotion work, and public activism, Streisand lastingly affects the world, rousing others to join her in the battle for an all the more, impartial, and manageable future.

7.2 Altruistic Work

Barbra Streisand's beneficent work traverses a great many drives and associations, mirroring her obligation to civil rights, philanthropy, and the improvement of society. Throughout her famous lifetime, Streisand has utilized her foundation, impact, and monetary assets to help causes that line up with her qualities and convictions. Here is a definite gander at Streisand's beneficent work:

1. Medical Care Drives: Streisand has been a noticeable ally of medical services drives, especially in the space of clinical exploration, ladies' wellbeing, and coronary illness counteraction. She has given a huge number of dollars to clinical examination establishments, medical clinics, and medical care associations, subsidizing earth-shattering exploration and giving basic assets to propel the field of medication. Streisand's help for medical care drives has assisted with working on clinical consideration, saving lives, and advancing better well-being results for people and networks all over the planet.

2. Instruction and Education Projects: Streisand is an enthusiastic supporter of schooling and proficiency,

perceiving the extraordinary force of figuring out how to change lives and fabricate more grounded networks. She has given to educational programs, libraries, and schools, funding scholarships, providing resources, and encouraging literacy programs for adults and children alike. Streisand's help for instruction and proficiency programs has assisted with further developing admittance to quality training, extending learning amazing open doors, and enabling people to arrive at their maximum capacity.

3. Expressions and Culture: Streisand has for quite some time been a hero of human expression, perceiving their significance in improving lives, encouraging imagination, and advancing social getting it. She has given money to museums, cultural institutions, and arts organizations to support projects that help underserved communities get access to the arts, promote arts education, and protect cultural heritage. Streisand's help for expressions and culture has assisted with saving imaginative practices, rousing people in the future of craftsmen, and advancing the worth of inventiveness and articulation in the public arena.

4. Natural Preservation: Streisand is a vocal promoter of ecological preservation and supportability, perceiving the pressing need to safeguard the planet and save regular assets for people in the future. She has given to natural

associations, preservation endeavors, and environmental change drives, financing projects that address ecological difficulties, advance sustainable power and safeguard jeopardized species and biological systems. Streisand's support for environmental preservation has contributed to global environmental awareness, action, and environmental stewardship.

5. Civil rights and Compassionate Causes: Streisand has been an eager promoter of civil rights and helpful purposes, utilizing her foundation to stand in opposition to unfairness, imbalance, and segregation. She has given to associations that work to progress social liberties, advance racial and orientation balance, and offer help to minimized and weak populaces. Streisand's help for civil rights and compassionate causes has assisted with intensifying underestimated voices, advocating for change, and making an all the more impartial society for all.

By and large, Barbra Streisand's beneficent work mirrors her profoundly held upsides of empathy, equity, and social obligation. Through her liberal gifts, support endeavors, and public activism, Streisand lastingly affects the world, rousing others to join her in the battle for an all the more, fair, and humane future.

CHAPTER 8: AWARDS AND HONORS

Throughout her illustrious career, Barbra Streisand has received numerous awards and honors that recognize her extraordinary talent, versatility, and contributions to the entertainment industry. From renowned industry honors to lifetime accomplishment grants, Streisand's prize bureau is loaded with distinctions that mirror her perseverance through her influence on music, film, and performing expressions. Here is a point by point take gander at a portion of the honors and praises Streisand has gotten all through her profession:

1. Institute Grants (Oscars): Two Academy Awards have been presented to Streisand, one for her performance in the 1968 film "Funny Girl." She won the Oscar for Best Entertainer for her depiction of Fanny Brice, making her the solitary entertainer to win both a Tony and an Oscar for a similar job. Streisand has also been up for several other Oscars, including Best Original Song for "Evergreen" from "A Star Is Born" (1976).

2. Grammy Grants: Streisand has won eight Grammy Grants throughout her profession, including Collection of the Year for "The Barbra Streisand Collection" (1963) and Record of the Year for "Affection Topic from A Star

Is Conceived (Evergreen)" (1977). She has likewise gotten various selections in different classifications, displaying her flexibility as an entertainer and mediator of melody.

3. Tony Grants: Streisand won a Tony Grant for Best Entertainer in a Melodic for her Broadway debut in "Entertaining Young Lady" (1964), procuring rave surveys for her notorious exhibition as Fanny Brice. She likewise received an Exceptional Tony Grant for Star of the 10 Years in 1970, perceiving her colossal commitment to the Broadway stage.

4. Brilliant Globe Grants: Streisand has won five Brilliant Globe Grants through her profession, remembering Best Entertainer for a Movie - Melodic or Parody for "Interesting Young Lady" (1968) and "How We Were" (1973). She has additionally received the Cecil B. DeMille Grant for Lifetime Accomplishment in 2000, respecting her exceptional commitments to the universe of diversion.

5. The Kennedy Center Award: Streisand was granted the Kennedy Place Respect in 2008, perceiving her lifetime of creative accomplishment and social effect. The lofty honor celebrates people who have made critical commitments to American culture through performing expressions, and Streisand's enlistment into

this regarded bunch is a demonstration of her perseverance through inheritance as an entertainer, chef, and humanitarian.

6. Freedom Medal from the President: Streisand was granted the Official Decoration of Opportunity, the most noteworthy non-military personnel honor in the US, by President Barack Obama in 2015. The decoration perceives people who have made extraordinary commitments to the security or public interests of the US, world harmony, social or other critical public or confidential undertakings. Streisand's receipt of this lofty honor features her impact and effect as a craftsman, extremist, and compassionate.

In general, Barbra Streisand's honors and praises are a demonstration of her unrivaled ability, flexibility, and getting through influence on the universe of diversion. From her noteworthy exhibitions in front of an audience and screen to her support for social causes and magnanimous undertakings, Streisand's heritage as a genuine symbol of human expression will keep on moving for ages to come.

8.1 Grammy Grants

Barbra Streisand's Grammy Grants are a demonstration of her striking ability, flexibility, and getting through influence on the music business. Throughout her famous lifetime, Streisand has gathered a sum of eight Grammy Grants, spreading over different classifications and types. Here is a nitty gritty gander at Streisand's Grammy wins:

1. Award for Best Album: Streisand won the lofty Collection of the Year grant for "The Barbra Streisand Collection" in 1963. This presentation collection shot Streisand to fame and exhibited her exceptional vocal reach and interpretive ability, acquiring basic recognition and business achievement.

2. Best Vocal Performance by a Female: Streisand has won the Grammy Grant for Best Female Vocal Execution multiple times through her profession. She won this honor for her exhibitions on tunes, for example, "Individuals" (1964), "I Go by Barbra" (1965), "Evergreen (Love Subject from A Star Is Conceived)" (1977), and "You Don't Bring Me Blossoms" (1979) (a two-part harmony with Neil Jewel).

3. Best Female Pop Vocal Performance: In 1977, Streisand's performance of "Evergreen (Love Theme from A Star Is Born)" earned her the Grammy Award for Best Pop Vocal Performance, Female. This notorious melody, composed for the film "A Star Is Conceived," became one of Streisand's unique hits and procured her both basic praise and business achievement.

4. Best Conventional Pop Vocal Collection: Throughout her career, Streisand has won the Grammy Award for Best Traditional Pop Vocal Album twice. She won this honor for her collections "The Broadway Collection" in 1986 and "Back to Broadway" in 1994, the two of which displayed Streisand's excellent ability to decipher exemplary Broadway principles.

5. Lifetime Accomplishment Grant: Notwithstanding her individual Grammy wins, Streisand has gotten the Grammy Lifetime Accomplishment Grant, respecting her exceptional commitments to the universe of music and amusement. This esteemed honor perceives Streisand's perseverance through influence as an entertainer, entertainer, and social symbol, hardening her inheritance as one of the best voices ever.

Generally, Barbra Streisand's Grammy Grants are a demonstration of her unmatched ability, flexibility, and enduring effect on the music business. From her noteworthy presentation collection to her notorious exhibitions in film and front of an audience, Streisand's Grammy wins commend her phenomenal profession and persevering through heritage as a genuine symbol of human expression.

8.2 Foundation Grants

Barbra Streisand's Foundation Grants, generally known as Oscars, are a demonstration of her excellent ability, flexibility, and perseverance through her her influence on the entertainment world. The Academy of Motion Picture Arts and Sciences has honored Streisand for her work in front of and behind the camera. Here is a definite glance at Streisand's Institute Grants:

1. Best Entertainer: Streisand won the Foundation Grant for Best Entertainer for her notorious depiction of Fanny Brice in the 1968 film "Amusing Young Lady." This cutting-edge job sent off Streisand to superstardom and procured her far-reaching approval for her enamoring execution, surprising performing voice, and evident allure. With her win, Streisand became the first and only performer to win an Oscar for her first leading role in a film.

2. Favorite Original Song: Streisand won the Foundation Grant for Best Unique Melody for "Evergreen (Love Topic from A Star Is Conceived)" in 1977. This immortal ditty, which Streisand co-composed and performed for the film "A Star Is Conceived," became one of her unique hits and procured her basic praise and

business achievement. Streisand's success further set her status as a multi-gifted craftsman and established her place in Hollywood history.

Notwithstanding her singular Oscar wins, Streisand has likewise gotten a few selections for her work as an entertainer, chief, and maker. She is admired and respected by her peers and fans alike for her contributions to film. Streisand's Foundation Grants are a demonstration of her unprecedented ability, flexibility, and getting through influence on the universe of the film, setting her inheritance as one of the best entertainers ever.

8.3 Other Awards

Barbra Streisand has won numerous other prestigious awards throughout her long career. These awards include the Grammy and Academy Awards. Her extraordinary talent, versatility, and lasting influence on the entertainment industry are recognized with these awards. Here is an itemized take-a-gander at a portion of different acknowledge received by Streisand:

1. The Tonys: Streisand won a Tony Grant for Best Entertainer in a Melodic for her Broadway debut in "Entertaining Young Lady" in 1964. She likewise got an Extraordinary Tony Grant for Star of the Ten Years in 1970, perceiving her massive commitment to the Broadway stage.

2. The Golden Globes: Throughout her career, Streisand has won five Golden Globe Awards, including Best Actress in a Musical or Comedy Film for "Funny Girl" (1968) and "The Way We Were" (1973). She additionally received the Cecil B. DeMille Grant for Lifetime Accomplishment in 2000, respecting her remarkable commitments to the universe of amusement.

3. Kennedy Center Distinctions: Streisand was granted the Kennedy Place Praises in 2008, perceiving her lifetime of creative accomplishment and social effect. People who have made significant contributions to American culture through the performing arts are honored with this prestigious title.

4. Official Award of Opportunity: Streisand was granted the Official Award of Opportunity, the most elevated non-military personnel honor in the US, by President Barack Obama in 2015. The award perceives people who have made remarkable commitments to the security or public interests of the US, world harmony, social, or other huge public or confidential undertakings.

5. Grammy Award for Lifetime Achievement: Streisand has won individual Grammys as well as the Grammy Lifetime Achievement Award for her extraordinary contributions to the music and entertainment industries. Streisand's legacy as a singer, performer, and cultural icon is honored with this prestigious award.

6. Hollywood Stroll of Distinction: Streisand was regarded with a star on the Hollywood Stroll of Notoriety in 1976, perceiving her commitments to media outlets. Situated on Hollywood Road, Streisand's star is an image of her enduring heritage and impact in Hollywood.

In general, Barbra Streisand's different acknowledgments are a demonstration of her unmatched ability, flexibility, and enduring effect on the universe of diversion. Streisand's legacy as a true icon of the arts will continue to inspire generations to come, from her groundbreaking performances on stage and screen to her advocacy for social causes and philanthropic endeavors.

CHAPTER 9: LATER PROFESSION

Barbra Streisand's later profession has been portrayed as proceeding with progress, advancement, and creative investigation across numerous mediums. While she has kept a lower profile as far as film appearances and live exhibitions lately, Streisand's impact and effect on media outlets remained areas of strength as could be expected. An in-depth look at Streisand's later work can be found here:

1. Music Deliveries: Streisand has kept on delivering collections and singles through her later profession, displaying her momentous vocal ability and imaginative adaptability. She has investigated a great many melodic kinds, from pop and jazz to Broadway guidelines and contemporary hits. Streisand's later collections incorporate "Love Is the Response" (2009), "Accomplices" (2014), and "Walls" (2018), every one of which got basic praise and business achievement.

2. Show Exhibitions: While Streisand has performed fewer live shows lately, she has kept on charming crowds with intermittent exhibitions and unique appearances. Fans from all over the world flock to her live concerts to experience her legendary voice and

captivating stage presence. presence. Streisand's later shows have included a blend of exemplary hits, fan-top choices, and new material, pleasing crowds with her immortal ability and mystique.

3. Coordinating and Creating: Streisand has moved her concentration background jobs as of late, coordinating and creating movies and TV projects. She has helmed a few acclaimed films, including "The Sovereign of Tides" (1991) and "The Mirror Has Two Countenances" (1996), procuring acclaim for her capable course and narration. Streisand's later ventures mirror her obligation to investigate complex subjects and human connections on screen.

4. Activism and charitable giving: Streisand stays dynamic in charity and activism, utilizing her foundation to advocate for social causes and advance positive change on the planet. Through her magnanimous establishment, The Streisand Establishment, she keeps on supporting a great many causes, including schooling, ladies' freedoms, medical care, and the climate. Compassion, justice, and social responsibility are reflected in Streisand's commitment to making a difference in the world.

5. Heritage and Impact: Streisand's later vocation is a demonstration of her perseverance through inheritance

and impact in media outlets. As one of the most notable and adaptable craftsmen ever, Streisand's effect can be felt in each side of the music, film, and theater universes. Her enduring talent, ground-breaking accomplishments, and unwavering dedication to her craft continue to inspire and influence audiences and artists alike, securing her place among entertainment legends for future generations.

By and large, Barbra Streisand's later vocation mirrors her continuous obligation to creative greatness, social activism, and charity. Streisand's legacy as one of the greatest artists of all time is solidified by the fact that even though she has reduced the number of times she performs and appears in public in recent years, her influence and impact on the entertainment industry remain as profound as ever.

9.1 Proceeded with Outcome in Music and Film

Notwithstanding downsizing her public appearances and exhibitions as of late, Barbra Streisand has kept on getting a charge out of progress in both music and film, showing her perseverance through ability, flexibility, and social significance. Here is a nitty gritty gander at Streisand's proceeded with progress in music and film:

1. Music: Streisand's music vocation has stayed dynamic and powerful, with with arrival of new collections and singles that feature her wonderful vocal ability and imaginative adaptability. She has investigated different kinds, from pop and jazz to Broadway principles and contemporary hits, proceeding to dazzle crowds with her emotive exhibitions and strong narrating. Reaffirming her status as one of the greatest vocalists of all time, Streisand's subsequent albums, "Love Is the Answer" (2009), "Partners" (2014), and "Walls" (2018), have received both critical acclaim and commercial success.

2. Film: Streisand's commitments to the movie have likewise gone on lately yet in addition to the background jobs as a chief and maker. She has been praised for her skillful direction, nuanced storytelling, and capacity to

bring complex characters to life on screen in films like "The Prince of Tides" (1991) and "The Mirror Has Two Faces" (1996). Streisand's later undertakings mirror her obligation to investigate subjects of adoration, family, and human connections in provocative and genuinely full ways, solidifying her heritage as a visionary movie producer.

3. Inheritance and Impact: Streisand's proceeded with progress in music and film is a demonstration of her perseverance through inheritance and impact in media outlets. As one of the most notable and flexible craftsmen ever, Streisand's effect can be felt in each side of the music, film, and theater universes. Her enduring talent, ground-breaking accomplishments, and unwavering dedication to her craft continue to inspire and influence audiences and artists alike, securing her place among entertainment legends for future generations.

Generally speaking, Barbra Streisand's proceeded with outcome in music and film is a demonstration of her continuous obligation to creative greatness, development, and narrating. While she might have moved her concentration to the background jobs lately, Streisand's impact and effect on the universe of diversion stay as significant as could be expected, cementing her inheritance as one of the best craftsmen ever.

9.2 Striking Activities

Barbra Streisand's profession is set apart by a large number of eminent ventures crossing music, film, and theater. These tasks feature her amazing ability, flexibility, and perseverance through her influence on media outlets. Here is a nitty gritty gander at a portion of Streisand's most striking tasks:

1. " Amusing Young lady" (1968): In the film adaptation of the Broadway musical "Funny Girl," Streisand played the legendary comedian and singer Fanny Brice. This was her breakthrough role. Streisand's exhibition procured her the Foundation Grant for Best Entertainer, making her the sole entertainer to win an Oscar for her film debut in a main job. Her version of notorious tunes like "Don't Spoil My Otherwise Good Vibes" and "Individuals" became moment works of art, cementing her status as a hotshot.

2. " How We Were" (1973): Streisand featured inverse Robert Redford in this heartfelt show, depicting the perplexing connection between two people with differentiating political convictions. The film's signature melody, likewise named "How We Were," became one of Streisand's particular hits and won her the Grammy

Grant for Best Female Pop Vocal Execution. The film stays a cherished work of art, commended for its strong narrating and strong exhibitions.

3. " A Star Is Conceived" (1976): Streisand featured inverse Kris Kristofferson in this melodic show, depicting a gifted vocalist musician on the ascent to notoriety. Streisand's presentation procured her basic praise and a Brilliant Globe Grant for Best Entertainer, while the film's soundtrack created the Foundation Grant-winning melody "Evergreen (Love Topic from A Star Is Conceived)." Streisand's depiction of the aggressive and versatile Esther Hoffman has become perhaps her most famous job.

4. " Yentl" (1983): Based on Isaac Bashevis Singer's short story "Yentl the Yeshiva Boy," this musical drama starred Streisand, who also directed, produced, co-wrote, and starred. The film recounts the narrative of a youthful Jewish lady who masks herself as a man to seek after her enthusiasm for learning and strict review. Streisand's diverse job as chief, maker, and star exhibited her ability and vision behind the camera, procuring her basic recognition and various honors.

5. " 1991's "The Prince of Tides": Streisand coordinated and featured in this heartfelt show, given the original by Pat Conroy. The film recounts the narrative of a pained

man who looks for help from his sister's specialist, prompting an excursion of self-disclosure and mending. Streisand's delicate heading and nuanced execution procured her basic recognition and Foundation Grant designations for Best Picture and Best Entertainer.

6. " Accomplices" (2014): Streisand's two part harmonies collection "Accomplices" highlights joint efforts with probably the greatest names in music, including Billy Joel, Stevie Marvel, and Elvis Presley. The collection appeared at number one on the Bulletin 200 graph, making Streisand the main craftsman to have a main collection in every one of the most recent sixty years. " Partners" was well-received by critics and consolidated Streisand's status as a music icon.

These prominent ventures address simply a small portion of Barbra Streisand's diverse vocation, which traverses more than sixty years and keeps on moving crowds all over the planet. Streisand's legacy as one of the greatest entertainers of all time has been established by her ground-breaking performances, inventive storytelling, and lasting influence.

9.3 Inheritance and Effect

Barbra Streisand's inheritance and effect on the universe of diversion are unlimited, traversing north of sixty years and impacting the ages of specialists and crowds the same. From her weighty accomplishments in music, film, and theater to her activism and altruism, Streisand's commitments have made a permanent imprint on the social scene. Here is a definite glance at Streisand's perseverance through inheritance and effect:

1. Melodic Trailblazer: Streisand's groundbreaking performances, inventive interpretations, and exceptional vocal talent revolutionized the music industry. Her particular voice, portrayed by its lucidity, range, and profound profundity, set another norm for vocal greatness and roused innumerable artists across classes. Streisand's famous accounts, including hits like "Individuals," "How We Were," and "Evergreen (Love Subject from A Star Is Conceived)," keep on reverberating with crowds overall and stay immortal works of art.

2. Exploring Entertainer: Streisand's effect on the universe of film and theater is similarly significant, with a profession that remembers notorious exhibitions for

motion pictures like "Interesting Young Lady," "How We Were," and "A Star Is Conceived." She broke obstructions as one of the primary female jokesters to make standard progress and acquired basic recognition for her emotional jobs, demonstrating her adaptability as an entertainer. Streisand's depiction of mind-boggling, multi-faceted characters prepared for people in the future of ladies in film and theater.

3. Visionary Chief and Maker: Streisand's gifts reach out past the stage and screen to the background jobs as a chief and maker. She has helmed a few acclaimed films, including "Yentl" and "The Sovereign of Tides," exhibiting her capable heading, nuanced narrating, and capacity to rejuvenate strong stories on screen. Streisand's commitments as a producer have gained her acknowledgment and appreciation from her friends, setting her status as a visionary in the business.

4. Social Symbol and Lobbyist: Streisand's influence extends beyond the entertainment industry to social and political activism, where she has used her platform to advocate for causes she believes in, such as women's rights, LGBTQ+ rights, healthcare, education, and environmental conservation. Streisand's influence extends beyond the entertainment industry. Through her charity, promotion work, and public activism, Streisand has brought issues to light about significant issues and

propelled positive change on the planet. Her obligation to civil rights and philanthropic causes mirrors her profoundly held upsides of sympathy, compassion, and fairness.

5. Getting through Motivation: Streisand's inheritance as a craftsman, lobbyist, and helpful keeps on rousing ages of fans and admirers all over the planet. For aspiring artists and activists alike, her timeless music, memorable performances, and unwavering dedication to her craft serve as a source of inspiration and empowerment. Streisand's impact rises above age and social limits, making a permanent imprint on the hearts and brains of millions.

By and large, Barbra Streisand's inheritance and effect are a demonstration of her unrivaled ability, flexibility, and perseverance through obligation to greatness. As one of the best performers ever, Streisand's commitments to music, film, and theater have molded the social scene and left a permanent engraving on the world, guaranteeing her spot in the pantheon of amusement legends for a long time into the future.

CONCLUSION

Barbra Streisand's remarkable vocation is a demonstration of the force of ability, constancy, and imaginative vision. From her modest starting points in Brooklyn, New York, to becoming quite possibly one of the most notorious and persuasive figures in diversion history, Streisand has pioneered a path of unmatched achievement and made a permanent imprint on the universe of music, film, and theater.

Through her six-very long-term vocation, Streisand has broken unattainable ranks, and broken records, and acquired innumerable honors, including numerous Grammy Grants, Institute Grants, and Brilliant Globe Grants. Her exceptional vocal ability, flexible acting abilities, and visionary filmmaking have enthralled crowds all over the planet and propelled ages of craftsmen and admirers.

Past her accomplishments at the center of attention, Streisand's inheritance stretches out to her activism and charity, where she has utilized her foundation to advocate for civil rights, fairness, and philanthropic causes. Her obligation to affect the planet mirrors her profoundly held upsides of sympathy, compassion, and strengthening.

As Barbra Streisand's vocation proceeds to motivate and impact, her immortal music, vital exhibitions, and faithful devotion to greatness act as a wake-up call of the groundbreaking force of workmanship and the getting-through effect of a genuine social symbol.

In conclusion, Barbra Streisand's legacy is not only a testament to her unrivaled talent and accomplishments but also to her resilience, honesty, and unwavering dedication to improving the world. Her impact will keep on reverberating for a long time into the future, guaranteeing that her heritage stays scratched in the records of diversion history forever.

www.ingramcontent.com/pod-product-compliance
Lightning Source LLC
Chambersburg PA
CBHW071058290526
45795CB00004B/1556